Teaching
Literary Elements
Using Poetry

PAUL B. JANECZKO

New York · Toronto · London · Auckland · Sydney
Mexico City · New Delhi · Hong Kong · Buenos Aires

Teaching
Resources

Dedication

For the next generation of writers and readers,
especially my grandnieces and grandnephews:
Drew, Jessica, and Jacob; Derek and Benjamin; Jonathan and Juliet; Zoe and Cacie.
May they be filled with loving-kindness.

CREDITS

Page 20: "Enchantment" by Joanne Ryder. Copyright © 2003 by Joanne Ryder. Reprinted by permission of the poet.

Page 25: "Jim" from *Bronzeville Boys and Girls* by Gwendolyn Brooks. Original copyright © 1956; published by Amistad, an imprint of HarperCollins; copyright © 2007.

Page 30: "Birdfoot's Grampa" from *Entering Onondaga* by Joseph Bruchac. Copyright © 1978 by Joseph Bruchac. Reprinted by permission of Barbara Kouts, literary agent for the poet.

Page 35: "Quilt" from *A Suitcase of Seaweed* by Janet S. Wong. Copyright © 1996 by Janet S. Wong. Reprinted by permission of the poet.

Page 41: "Mary Todd Lincoln Speaks of Her Son's Death, 1862" by Paul B. Janeczko. Copyright © 2007 by Paul B. Janeczko. Originally appeared in *Our White House: Looking In, Looking Out*; published by Candlewick Press. Reprinted by permission of the poet.

Page 45: "Concrete Mixers" from *8 A.M. Shadows* by Patricia Hubbell. Copyright © 1965 by Patricia Hubbell; published by Atheneum.

Page 51: "Crumble!" from *Earthshake: Poems From the Ground Up* by Lisa Westberg Peters. Text copyright © 2003 by Lisa Westberg Peters; published by Greenwillow Books, an imprint of HarperCollins.

Page 55: "Toby Twits Tina" from *Alpha Beta Chowder* by Jeanne Steig. Copyright © 1994; published by HarperCollins.

Page 59: "Washing Machine" from *A Rumpus of Rhymes: A Book of Noisy Poems* by Bobbi Katz; published by Dutton Children's Books. Copyright © 2001 by Bobbi Katz, who controls all rights. Used by permission of the poet.

Page 64: "Junkyard Dog" from *It's About Dogs*; poems by Tony Johnston. Copyright © 2000 by The Living Trust of Tony Johnston. Reprinted by permission of Houghton Mifflin Harcourt Publishing Company. All rights reserved.

Page 69: "Riding the Wind" by Doris Bircham. Copyright © by Doris Bircham.

Every effort has been made to secure permission for the use of all copyrighted material.
The publisher will gladly make any necessary corrections in future printings.

Edited by Mela Ottaiano
Cover design and illustration by Brian LaRossa
Interior design by Sydney Wright
ISBN: 978-0-545-19572-0

Copyright © 2014 by Paul B. Janeczko

Illustrations copyright © 2014 by Scholastic Inc.
All rights reserved.
Published by Scholastic Inc.

3 4 5 6 7 8 9 10   40   21 20 19 18 17

Contents

Contents *(continued)*

REPRODUCIBLE ACTIVITY PAGES

Contents *(continued)*

Introduction

Poetry is a part of any well-balanced English Language Arts instruction. It is also a perfect avenue for teaching literary elements. Since poems are typically shorter than other types of literature, you can easily focus on particular elements within the text, without losing sight of the poem as a whole.

Poems are also a natural fit for close-reading lessons. As students must read carefully and multiple times to better understand a poem, they learn to analyze craft and structure, word choices, how language conveys mood and meaning, and so on, along the way. (See the tips on page 10 for a successful close-reading routine.)

Through the close-reading lessons and engaging activities in this book, students gain a solid understanding of key literary elements, including plot, character, setting, theme, figurative language, such as metaphor and simile, and more. Students can then apply this knowledge to help them identify these elements in all types of literature, allowing them a deeper comprehension of what they read—an important step in meeting higher standards and building college and career readiness.

From "The Golden Vanity," a traditional ballad, to "Riding the Wind," a lyric poem, the 12 poems selected to highlight the literary elements vary in length and poetic form. The following chart will help you see at a glance why they were chosen.

Poem	Literary Element	The Connection
"The Golden Vanity" Traditional Ballad	Plot	The ballad is one of the oldest poetic forms that tell a story. You'll note the narrative arc and the pattern throughout this poem.
"Enchantment" by Joanne Ryder	Setting	Ryder employs precise language in this lyric poem to capture a specific setting, providing vivid details of both time and place.
"Jim" by Gwendolyn Brooks	Character	Brooks uses clear examples in this poem to show the reader what sort of character Jim has.
"Birdfoot's Grampa" by Joseph Bruchac	Theme	Bruchac relies on a very short narrative poem to examine the theme of what's important to the narrator's grandfather.
"Quilt" by Janet S. Wong	Symbolism	Wong's free-verse poem shows how a poet can use something concrete to stand for a larger issue or concept.
"Mary Todd Lincoln Speaks of Her Son's Death, 1862" by Paul B. Janeczko	Metaphor	This poem utilizes three direct comparisons to measure the grief that Mrs. Lincoln felt at the death of her son.
"Concrete Mixers" by Patricia Hubbell	Simile	This poem is also built on comparisons, with similes spread throughout.
"Crumble!" by Lisa Westberg Peters	Personification	In this poem of address, Peters speaks to sandstone, as if it were a person, in the process giving us a geology lesson.
"Toby Twits Tina" by Jeanne Steig	Alliteration	This short, humorous poem is a good example of how important the sounds of words in a poem can be, especially the initial consonants.
"Washing Machine" by Bobbi Katz	Onomatopoeia	In this mask poem, Katz pretends she is a washing machine and speaks from that point of view, using lots of washing-machine–like sound words.
"Junkyard Dog" by Tony Johnston	Mood	In this poem, Johnston creates a scene and a feeling through the use of many harsh and menacing words.
"Riding the Wind" by Doris Bircham	Poetic Patterns	Like the ballad in the first lesson, this lyric poem follows a pattern of stanza lengths and end rhymes.

Teaching Literary Elements Using Poetry © 2014 by Paul B. Janeczko • Scholastic Teaching Resources

How to Use This Book

You may use the lessons in this book in any order that suits your curriculum needs. Each lesson follows the same format. First, there is a **definition** of the literary element, followed by suggestions for how to **introduce the literary element** to kick off the lesson. Next, you'll find some key information to help you **introduce the poem** to the class.

A **vocabulary** box highlights various words and phrases students may find unfamiliar. Invite students to volunteer meanings of these words or have them look up definitions before reading the poem. While a brief dictionary session will likely clarify these terms and help students when they encounter them in the poem, you may want to encourage students to try to understand the words by using context clues.

Once it's time to **read the poem**, like most poets, I'm a firm believer in reading it aloud. When you do that, you can hear things in the poem that you might miss when you read it to yourself. So, I urge you to always give students the time and the opportunity to read and listen to the poems aloud. I provide poem-specific pointers to best engage the class.

Class discussion suggestions and other activity ideas to use **after reading** will help students better grasp the concept of the literary element by closely examining how it appears in the poem—and enhances it. There is also a list of other great poems for teaching that literary element.

Then, through a **writing activity**, students apply their knowledge of the literary element to their own writing. Finally, there are ideas to help you **extend the lesson**.

You will find **reproducible activity pages**—at least one per lesson—in the back of the book. Often these pages are graphic organizers, which will help students keep track of their thinking and boost their understanding of the literary element. Many are versatile; you can use them for multiple lessons and multiple purposes. In addition, there is a glossary of key terms, which will help students in their study of literary elements.

Close-Reading Routine

Since poetry comes in so many forms and its layers of meaning range from simple wordplay to explorations of abstract thoughts, students may benefit from using a close-reading routine when they encounter poems of greater complexity. A complex poem may require students to use inference to understand its meaning—and it may have more than one meaning. The poem may use figurative language, unfamiliar meanings of words, or even assume some background knowledge. If this is the case, recommend the following strategies to students:

- Preview the poem. Reading the title and scanning the poem to look for a structure can help set the stage for the first reading.

- Read the poem once to get its gist. This step will help bring attention to any tricky vocabulary or concepts.

- Reread the poem. This time, slow down; read carefully and stay focused. Now is a good time to monitor understanding. It may be necessary to read a poem several times.

- Take notes and summarize. Keep track of repeated words or phrases and spot patterns. Summarize key points in each stanza. Write questions and make connections between ideas.

- Think about it. Read between the lines. What is the poet saying in the poem? Do you agree or disagree with the ideas expressed in the poem?

Teaching Literary Elements Using Poetry © 2014 by Paul B. Janeczko • Scholastic Teaching Resources

LESSONS

Plot

Teaching Literary Elements Using Poetry © 2014 by Paul B. Janeczko • Scholastic Teaching Resources

"The Golden Vanity"
Traditional Ballad

Introducing the Literary Element

Plot is the series of events or situations in a narrative. Usually there are cause-effect relationships between some of the events in a story.

Ask for volunteers to summarize, or tell the main parts of, a story the class might know. For example, one student may tell the story of "Little Red Riding Hood" or another fairy tale. Another might summarize a novel, such as *Because of Winn Dixie* by Kate DiCamillo. After a few students have had the chance to give a plot summary of various stories, you can let them know that they have just described the main elements of a plot. Then, write the definition of plot on the board.

At this point, it's important that students understand the cause-effect relationship between events in a plot. You can return to one of the fairy tale summaries and ask students to identify some of the cause-effect connections at work in that story. For example, Little Red Riding Hood goes to her Granny's house because she wants to visit. Because she goes into the house, she is confronted by the Big Bad Wolf, and so on.

Have students work in groups of two or three. Distribute a copy of the **Organizer: Plot Boxes** activity page (page 75) to each student. (You may need to print extra organizers for students who need more than 10 boxes to summarize a plot.) Each group should choose one story and write a plot summary in their organizers. If necessary, suggest titles of books they have read in class. Whenever students notice a cause-

effect relationship, they will draw an arrow from the "cause box" to the "effect box." Not all of the boxes will need to be linked in this way, and some effects may become causes that lead to another effect.

After the class has had time to work on the organizers, ask each group to report on its story and identify any cause-effect relationships it included. By the time all the groups have reported, the class should have a good understanding of what makes up a plot of a narrative

Introducing the Poem

Simply put, a ballad is a story in song. There are variations in the form, but you can usually count on a ballad to tell a story, most often in the third person, including a lot of dialogue. This version of "The Golden Vanity" is just one of many variations of the British ballad. Other versions feature different settings or enemies, but the plot of betrayal is basically the same. Students need not know what the Lowland sea is or when the British fought the Turks. All they need to know is that the cabin boy volunteers to sink an enemy ship and he is betrayed by his captain.

≫ Vocabulary ≪

Here are a few words that students may not know: *gallant, auger, bored, mocked, port, messmates, hammock.*

Reading the Poem

Since ballads were originally sung, they are performance poems. If you want to let the class hear the ballad being sung, search the Internet to find singers and groups performing this ballad. You could also let students perform the poem by reading it in several parts. The simplest way for them to read the poem is to have one student read the narrative part and two other students read the parts of the cabin boy and the captain. To make the reading more dramatic, you can have the narrative parts read by a chorus of three or four students, or more.

Teaching Literary Elements Using Poetry © 2014 by Paul B. Janeczko • Scholastic Teaching Resources

"The Golden Vanity"
Traditional Ballad

There was a gallant ship, a gallant ship was she,
And the name of the ship was *The Golden Vanity*
And they feared she would be taken by the Turkish enemy
    As she sailed upon the Lowland, Lowland, Lowland,
    As she sailed upon the Lowland sea.

Then up came a little cabin boy, and thus spoke he,
Speaking to the captain, "What will you give to me
If I swim alongside of the Turkish enemy
    And sink her in the Lowland, Lowland, Lowland,
    And sink her in the Lowland sea?"

"I'll give you an estate in the North Countrie,
And my one and only daughter your lovely bride shall be,
If you'll swim alongside of the Turkish enemy
    And sink her in the Lowland, Lowland, Lowland,
    And sink her in the Lowland sea."

Then the boy made ready and overboard sprang he,
And swam alongside of the Turkish enemy,
And with his auger sharp in her side he bored holes three,
    And he sunk her in the Lowland, Lowland, Lowland,
    He sunk her in the Lowland sea.

Then the boy swam around, and back again swam he,
And he called to the captain of *The Golden Vanity*
But the captain mocked, "You can drown for all of me!"
    And he left him in the Lowland, Lowland, Lowland
    He left him in the Lowland sea.

The boy swam around, he came to the port side,
He looked up at his messmates, and bitterly he cried:
"Oh, messmates, take me up, for I'm drifting with the tide,
    And I'm sinking in the Lowland, Lowland, Lowland,
    I'm sinking in the Lowland sea."

His messmates took him up, but on the deck he died,
And they sewed him in a hammock that was so large and wide.
They lowered him overboard, but he drifted with the tide,
    And he sank beneath the Lowland, Lowland, Lowland,
    He sank beneath the Lowland sea.

Teaching Literary Elements Using Poetry © 2014 by Paul B. Janeczko • Scholastic Teaching Resources

After Reading

When students have had a chance to read the poem over a couple of times, ask them to identify the important events in the story. Make a list of their responses on the board. They may see that each stanza in the poem contains a part of the plot. In other words, each stanza advances the narrative. After you have gotten a suitable list of plot events, ask students to connect the ones that are linked with a cause-effect relationship.

The next step in helping students understand plot is to have them put the plot events on a plot line that shows rising action, climax, and falling action. Distribute copies of the **Organizer: Plot Line** activity page (page 76) and have students try to fill it in using events from the ballad.

After students have had a chance to think about the order of events on their own, review the plot as a class.

Draw a plot line on the board (use a diagram that is similar to the one shown on the organizer). You might want to begin your discussion by asking students when the climax of the story occurs. This moment is the point of highest action in the story. The events prior to the climax lead up to it. The climax of this poem appears in the first line of the last stanza: "His messmates took him up, but on the deck he died." Ask students if they can see how the actions earlier in the poem lead to that point in the story. The events that come after the cabin boy's death constitute the falling action, or the tying up of loose ends, so to speak.

Students should make adjustments to their plot lines, as necessary, based on the class discussion. Encourage them to keep the organizer as a reference to use if they reread this poem or for the next time they try to identify plot events in another poem or story.

More Great Poems for Teaching Plot

"The Wreck of the Hesperus," Henry Wadsworth Longfellow

"John Henry," American ballad

"Annabel Lee," Edgar Allan Poe

Teaching Literary Elements Using Poetry © 2014 by Paul B. Janeczko • Scholastic Teaching Resources

Writing Activity

Students will write their own very short story in an eight-page mini-booklet. This activity will help students see how the plot of a story is made up of events or situations that are related to each other. Students may choose to retell a fairy tale, write an original fictional story, or relate a personal experience. Remind students that "The Golden Vanity" was comprised of a title and seven stanzas and point out that their stories should have a title and seven parts, each of which will go on a page of the mini-booklet. Have students start by writing drafts of the events they want to include in their booklets, then revising and rewriting the drafts so each of their stories has seven parts. As students are writing their stories, remind them that there should be a connection between each of the events and situations. They write their final copy in the booklet.

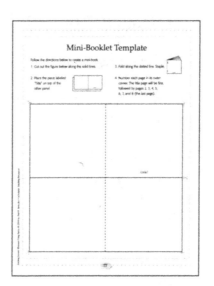

Distribute the **Mini-Booklet Template** (page 77) to students after each has drafted a story and is ready to write it in the booklet. Have them follow the directions on the template to create their own booklet.

If the class has never made booklets like this before, it might be helpful for you to show your own finished example so students will better understand your expectations.

Lesson Extensions

❀ Compare this version of "The Golden Vanity" with other versions of the ballad.

❀ Compare this ballad with another ballad.

❀ Explore the plots of other British and Scottish ballads in the *Child Ballads*, 305 ballads collected by Francis James Child.

Setting

"Enchantment"
Joanne Ryder

Introducing the Literary Element

Setting is where and when a poem or story takes place.

In some works of literature, a specific setting is central to the work. For example, the Harry Potter novels take place (mostly) at Hogwarts and because the location is so integral to the story, it's hard to imagine what would happen to Harry and his friends and foes in any other setting.

On the other hand, there are countless novels for young readers that take place in generic middle schools all over the country. In these the focus is less on setting than on what the characters do and how they grow over the course of the novel.

To begin an exploration of setting, have students work in groups of two or three. Give each student a copy of the **Organizer: Setting 1** activity page (page 78), on which to write information about the settings of novels they've read or movies they've seen. Students should specific in their descriptions.

When students have had time to discuss the organizer with their group, ask them to report to the class what they wrote on the organizers. Chances are students discovered that settings are more important to some stories than others. Summarize students' reports on the board or chart paper, so the class can see examples of how settings work in narratives that most of them will know.

Teaching Literary Elements Using Poetry © 2014 by Paul B. Janeczko • Scholastic Teaching Resources

Introducing the Poem

Part of what makes "Enchantment" such a wonderful poem is that Joanne Ryder doesn't try to do too much, and that is something that you should point out to your students. Young writers are often tempted to try to do too much, to take on a subject that is epic in scope when something much more limited is called for. For example, if students have recently experienced a blizzard, they might be motivated to write a poem about how it paralyzed the region. However, you might suggest they write a haiku or a tanka about snow stacked on a swing in the playground. After all, a vivid setting can be achieved using relatively few words.

Another element that makes "Enchantment" successful is the precision of the details that Ryder includes in the poem. As she carefully describes the setting—the family's porch on summer evenings—Ryder conveys a feeling of fondness for that special time and place. I especially like "in the patch of brightness/the lamp scatters on the floor." And can't you just picture the bugs "clinging to the screens" as they "watch our games/and listen to our talk till bedtime"? Ryder is able to notice these details and turn these phrases because she does what good poets do: poets pay attention. And that is a good lesson for young writers to learn.

⇒ Vocabulary ⇐

It's important that students understand the meaning of the title of the poem. Ask them to define *enchantment*. They might give examples of movies or books in which characters are enchanted, such as *Ella Enchanted* or the Harry Potter novels. The important thing for them to understand is the magical quality attached to that word. The setting of the poem—the porch on "warm summer nights"—is magical.

Reading the Poem

This is such a quiet poem that I'd suggest having one student read it aloud. The reader needs to convey the "spell" of the scene. You might want to add some lighting effects if you can because that element is important to the poem and its setting. Perhaps it would be effective if the lights went out near the end of the poem, leaving the performer to recite the final few lines in the dark.

Teaching Literary Elements Using Poetry © 2014 by Paul B. Janeczko • Scholastic Teaching Resources

"Enchantment"

Joanne Ryder

On warm summer nights
the porch becomes our living room
where Mama takes her reading
and Dad and I play games
in the patch of brightness
the lamp scatters on the floor.
From the darkness, others come—
small round bodies
clinging to the screens
which separate us
from the yard beyond.
Drawn to our light,
the June bugs watch our games
and listen to our talk till bedtime
when Mama darkens the porch
and breaks the spell
that holds them close to us.

Teaching Literary Elements Using Poetry © 2014 by Paul B. Janeczko • Scholastic Teaching Resources

After Reading

Have students reread "Enchantment" a few times and take note of any indications of setting. They can also take note of anything in it they don't understand and what they like about the poem.

Once they have had time to do this, you can begin a discussion. Ask students to think about what they know about the setting of the poem. We know the time—a warm summer night—and the place—"the porch becomes our living room." These are the basic *when* and *where* of the poem. But ask students to dig a little deeper into the setting. What other details do they notice? Give them a copy of the **Organizer: Setting 2** activity page (page 79) and ask them to list other details in the poem, such as Mama reading while the narrator and her father play games.

Ask students to look more carefully at the setting and pay attention to the language Ryder uses to set the scene. They should notice phrases such as "in the patch of brightness/the lamp scatters on the floor" and those "small round bodies/clinging to the screens."

More Great Poems for Teaching Setting

"A Room in the Past," Ted Kooser

"Dusk," Jim Harrison

"porches," Valerie Worth

Teaching Literary Elements Using Poetry © 2014 by Paul B. Janeczko • Scholastic Teaching Resources

Writing Activity

Have students write a short free-verse poem or a paragraph or two about a pleasant family scene they recall. It might be an everyday scene as in "Enchantment," a vacation scene, or a holiday scene. They might tell a simple story or simply describe the scene. Remind them to focus on the details that add to the setting in the scene—to convey a time and/or a place that they found "enchanting." It they can't quite get their thoughts into sentences, they can at least start with a brainstorming web where they list some of the elements that led to their feelings. Have them consider what made the situation enchanting or made them wish that it wouldn't end, whether there were other people involved or if they were alone, and so on.

Lesson Extensions

- Find a picture of a June bug. Does it change your feelings toward the poem to see what a June bug looks like? If so, how?

- Review the enchanting scene you described in the Writing Activity. Add a photo, drawing, or other artwork to enhance your written description.

Teaching Literary Elements Using Poetry © 2014 by Paul B. Janeczko • Scholastic Teaching Resources

Character

"Jim"

Gwendolyn Brooks

Introducing the Literary Element

A character is a person or other figure in a work of literature.

I'm a firm believer that character is the engine that drives good writing. Without strong, full characters, you'd still have a story, but chances are the emotional connection between a reader and the page will be missing—and the book ultimately unsatisfying.

Think about some of the novels, movies, plays, and TV shows that you enjoy. I'm willing to bet that you enjoy those works because you are interested in one of the characters. Sure, plot is important in fiction, but would you enjoy the work if you didn't have some sort of relationship with the characters? Whether in Hermione Granger or Katniss Everdeen, Huck Finn or Jane Eyre, it's all about a connection to the character. If they are deftly created and developed, we want to know—we have to know—what happens to them.

Distribute copies of the **Organizer: Character** activity page (page 80) to students. In the column on the left, each student should supply the names of stories, or any narrative literature, movies, or TV shows they enjoy. In the column on the right, they should list their favorite characters from each of the works. You could require students to make sure their lists include a novel or two. Encourage students to consider novels they've read that were not assignments for class.

After students have had time to fill out the organizers, ask each to report on one of the works included in his or her lists. Record students' observations on the board or chart paper. Although many of the same books and shows will appear in their lists, ask that each student not repeat a work already mentioned. This diversity will broaden the class list. Students will see that most of their favorites have strong characters: that, in fact, those characters are why they watch a show every week or continue reading a novel.

Introducing the Poem

As the title suggests, "Jim" is a poem about a character. By the end of the poem, we have a good idea what sort of person Jim is. He is kind and thoughtful in the way he acts when his "Mother-dear" is sick. We learn about his personality through his behavior.

When students read fiction in class, they should—as you have probably explained to them—appreciate how a writer makes a character come alive in a number of ways, including:

• Description of a character's appearance

• The way a character speaks

• Comments the author makes about him or her

• The way a character acts

Gwendolyn Brooks describes Jim's actions to inform us what sort of boy he is.

After discussing with students the ways an author creates a character, ask them to look at their organizers and describe how they get to know some of the characters on their lists. They should be able to come up with examples from most of the character development techniques mentioned above.

⇒ Vocabulary ⇐

Words that students may not know: *broth, tidied, tipping*. You could ask them what *tipping* means in the first line of the third stanza. Students may know *tipping* as the word to describe what their parents do when they pay the check in a restaurant. But in this case, *tipping* is used in the third stanza as shorthand for *tiptoeing*.

Reading the Poem

Because of the rhythm in the poem, as well as the rhyming lines, it strikes me as a poem that needs to be read smoothly and quickly; maybe accompanied by

Teaching Literary Elements Using Poetry © 2014 by Paul B. Janeczko • Scholastic Teaching Resources

"Jim"

Gwendolyn Brooks

There never was a nicer boy
Than Mrs. Jackson's Jim.
The sun should drop its greatest gold
On him.

Because, when Mother-dear was sick,
He brought her cocoa in.
And brought her broth, and brought her bread.
And brought her medicine.

And, tipping, tidied up her room.
And would not let her see
He missed his game of baseball
Terribly.

finger-snapping or soft hand-clapping to emphasize the rhythm. It can be effective when read by a single performer, perhaps with a background of snaps and/or claps. Or you might see what it sounds like when it is read by a chorus of six to eight students. There is a hushed quality to this poem that may be captured by a small chorus.

After Reading

Have students read the poem a few times. Discuss with them how Brooks shows us what sort of boy Jim Jackson is. To help students see how the poet creates a character, distribute **Organizer: Character Web** activity page (page 81), a brainstorming web with a large circle in the center where they can write JIM. Ask students to fill in the boxes at the ends of each line with something that shows them what sort of kid Jim is. By the time they have completed the organizer, they'll see that Brooks primarily uses actions to describe Jim's character.

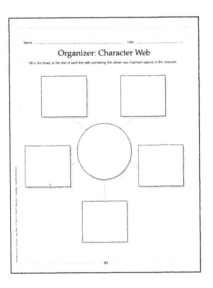

More Great Poems for Teaching Character

"Blubber Lips," Jim Daniels

"Speak Up," Janet S. Wong

"Friends in the Klan," Marilyn Nelson

Teaching Literary Elements Using Poetry © 2014 by Paul B. Janeczko • Scholastic Teaching Resources

Writing Activity

Again distribute copies of the **Organizer: Character Web** to students and ask them to sketch out some of the basics of a character of each own's creation. Make sure they understand that they won't have time to fully develop a character, only a few personality traits. As the class works on their character webs, you can reiterate the four ways that authors create characters (see page 24). You might jot them on the board as a quick reference. Students need not use all four techniques, but they should try to use two or three.

Once students have created their character webs, have them work in pairs. Can they offer some helpful suggestions that may enhance each partner's character? Are there items on their webs they'd like to reconsider?

Finally, ask each student to come up with a brief summary or outline of a story that would include his or her character. How about a story that includes that character as well as the one created by his or her partner?

Lesson Extensions

- Research Gwendolyn Brooks's background. Does her personal history provide more clues about the character Jim? Explain.

- Compare how character is portrayed in this poem with another poem about character, such as "Summertime Sharing" by Nikki Grimes or "Pet Rock" by Cynthia Rylant.

Theme

"Birdfoot's Grampa"

Joseph Bruchac

Introducing the Literary Element

Theme is the large view of life that a poet conveys in a poem.

No doubt you have discussed the notion of theme with your class when they read fiction. Begin your exploration of theme in poetry by distributing the **Organizer: Theme** activity page (page 82). Ask students to work in pairs to fill in the organizer with the titles of some of the fiction they've read. Partners should discuss and decide the theme of each narrative and write their ideas on the organizer.

Point out to students that the writer usually doesn't state the theme directly. It's up to readers to discover the theme for themselves. Students also need to understand that a theme is not a single word, like *war* or *love*. Such a single word can be a topic or a subject of a novel or poem. A theme is more involved than that, and I will say more about that in After Reading. But you should also remind students that a theme is more than just the "moral" of a story expressed in a trite expression, such as *Everything comes to she who waits* or *Hard work always pays off in the end.*

Teaching Literary Elements Using Poetry © 2014 by Paul B. Janeczko • Scholastic Teaching Resources

Introducing the Poem

Like the three poems in the preceding lessons, "Birdfoot's Grampa" tells a simple story. And as is the case with the previous poems, there's more to this poem than the simple story that it tells. The two characters in the poem are of different generations, so they look at the world from different points of view. And it is the contrast in the way they see the world that illuminates the theme, the poet's larger view of life.

In addition to being a good poem to illustrate theme, it builds off of the elements of literature that are covered in the first three poems: plot, setting, and character. So, while the main lesson for this poem is theme, it is, in a sense, a review of the earlier lessons. It affords a chance for you to show your students that good poems offer opportunities to study many of the elements of literature.

⇒ Vocabulary ⇐

While there's nothing very complicated about the language in "Birdfoot's Grampa," make sure students note some of the exquisite phrases that Joseph Bruchac includes in it, such as the metaphor in the first stanza: "leaping,/ live drops of rain." You may need to explain the unusual usages of words such as "live drops of rain" to describe leaping frogs, "a mist about his white hair" to describe the way the rain looked, "leathery" to describe hands, or "wet brown life" to describe muddy frogs.

Reading the Poem

Although a single reader could effectively read this poem, there is another approach that I would like to suggest. I see two parts to the poem: Birdfoot, who is narrating the poem, and Grampa. More specifically, the narrator (Birdfoot) reads all of the poem, except for the last two lines of the poem, which are spoken by Grampa. The readers you select for the voices of Birdfoot and Grampa need to be able to sound the part. By that I mean: for Birdfoot, who is exasperated with his eccentric grandfather, the reader should sound pleading; for Grampa, who—on the other hand—is smiling when he speaks the last seven words of the poem, the reader should sound mellow and patient.

Teaching Literary Elements Using Poetry © 2014 by Paul B. Janeczko • Scholastic Teaching Resources

"Birdfoot's Grampa"

Joseph Bruchac

The old man
must have stopped our car
two dozen times to climb out
and gather into his hands
the small toads blinded
by our lights and leaping,
live drops of rain.

The rain was falling,
a mist about his white hair
and I kept saying
you can't save them all,
accept it, get back in
we've got places to go.

But, leathery hands full
of wet brown life,
knee deep in the summer
roadside grass,
he just smiled and said
they have places to go to
too.

Teaching Literary Elements Using Poetry © 2014 by Paul B. Janeczko • Scholastic Teaching Resources

After Reading

Have students listen to the poem again. This time, invite different students to read "Birdfoot's Grampa" aloud to the class while the rest follows along. You can begin a discussion about the poem's theme once students have had the chance to read the poem a couple of times.

Distribute copies of the **Organizer: Plot Line** activity page (page 76, also used in Lesson 1) and ask students to fill out the plot diagram for this poem. Which lines of the poem are part of the rising action? Where is the turning point in the poem? Understanding the turning point of the poem is important in understanding its theme.

To determine and express the theme in "Birdfoot's Grampa," it is important to examine the language and the situation in the poem. An exploration of the structure of the poem is a place to start. As the stanzas suggest, the poem is organized in three parts that follow the narrative arc:

• Stanza 1 sets the scene and begins the narration.

• Stanza 2 introduces complications.

• Stanza 3 contrasts with the first two stanzas.

The *But* that starts the third stanza is the pivotal point of the poem because of the contradiction that it indicates. Stanza 2 ends with Birdfoot speaking:

> you can't save them all,
> accept it, get back in
> we've got places to go.

Then comes *But*, and the old man trying to pick up the small toads:

> he just smiled and said
> *they have places to go to*
> *too.*

From this rhetorical structure—action-reaction—we can figure that Bruchac's theme could be expressed something like this: *We need to pay attention to the small creature,* or *Even the small creatures deserve our respect.* We can believe that this theme—this larger, abstract idea—is how Bruchac was feeling when he wrote the poem. We can disagree, saying, *Oh, those small toads aren't that important.* Nevertheless that doesn't change the poem or the poet's theme in it. Do we know for sure what the poet was thinking when he wrote "Birdfoot's Grampa"? Of course not. Not without asking him. However, we can find evidence of the theme in the poem if we are thoughtful and attentive when we read it.

"Cottontail," George Bogin

"Famous," Naomi Shihab Nye

"Nothing Gold Can Stay," Robert Frost

Writing Activity

Bruchac's poem makes an eloquent plea for us to be more mindful of the small creatures of nature. "Birdfoot's Grampa" seems a fitting introduction for encouraging students to make some of their own nature observations and to use them to explore the same theme. Students can follow "Birdfoot's Grampa" as a model, writing a poem with three stanzas to convey the theme. If students would like to present the theme using a different writing form, or even tackle a different theme altogether, encourage them to do so.

Lesson Extensions

Read more poems by Joseph Bruchac and determine the themes. What do the themes have in common?

Bruchac is a part-Abenaki Indian writer and storyteller, who has published many books that feature his Native American heritage. Find out about other Native American writers. Look for similarities and differences in their world views and how these attitudes are expressed in their writing.

Teaching Literary Elements Using Poetry © 2014 by Paul B. Janeczko • Scholastic Teaching Resources

Symbolism

"Quilt"
Janet S. Wong

Introducing the Literary Element

Symbolism uses an object to stand for something larger than itself.

Let me clarify this simple definition by saying that the "something else" beyond the concrete object is usually an abstract idea or a system of ideas. We see symbols all around us. A common symbol is the American flag. It is, after all, just a piece of cloth with red and white stripes on it and 50 white stars on a field of blue. A glorious sight for many Americans, but still just a piece of cloth. However, it is what the flag symbolizes that gives it its importance. The flag is a symbol that stands for "something else beyond it." It stands for freedom and democracy. No wonder we show respect for these qualities when we recite the "Pledge of Allegiance" or sing "The Star Spangled Banner."

Religious symbols are also common symbols. The Christian cross, the Star of David, and the Yin and Yang are objects that represent complex spiritual and historical beliefs far beyond these symbols. Indeed, millions have died defending what the symbols represent.

Give each student a copy of the **Organizer: Symbolism** activity page (page 83), which asks students to list six symbols and explain the meaning of each. Discuss some basic symbols with the class to make sure that all students understand what kind of things they are expected to write on the organizer. Here are a few simple examples:

• heart: love

• skull and cross bones: poison

Teaching Literary Elements Using Poetry © 2014 by Paul B. Janeczko • Scholastic Teaching Resources

- dove: peace

- wedding ring: love and commitment

Ask students to supply a few other symbols, which you can write on the board. When you are sure they understand what sort of symbols you are looking for, give them some time to work on their organizers.

Introducing the Poem

From the first two lines of the poem, we know that Janet S. Wong is speaking metaphorically: *Our family/is a quilt.* Indeed, she has chosen an apt metaphor to describe her family, since a quilt is made up of patches of cloth that are stitched together to make a whole.

You might want to begin your exploration of the poem by making sure students know what a quilt is. Some may not know. Others may think it is another name for a heavy blanket or a thick comforter. They need to know that Wong is talking about the folk-art artifacts that are handmade by quilting groups. To make sure they get what a quilt is, you can share some pictures of quilts. It might also help to tell them a little bit about the quilting process, particularly how the pieces of the quilt often come from pieces of cloth that belonged to members of the family. For example, a square from a grandfather's shirt or a piece from a favorite doll's dress may find its way into a quilt.

⇒ Vocabulary ⇐

Words students may not know: *remnants, fraying.* I admire Wong's choice of words that reflect the overarching symbolism in the poem. Notice how the "odd remnants" are "patched together." The quilt contains threads that are fraying. Such word choice holds the poem together and lets the reader understand how Wong's metaphor is well chosen, her poem well executed.

Reading the Poem

This is quiet poem, but one that needs to be spoken with the pride the narrator has for her family. Even though the quilt includes "odd remnants," Wong believes it was "made to keep/its warmth."

Try this: have 12 students each read one line of the poem. Choose boys and girls, since different voices may bring out different textures from the poem. You

Teaching Literary Elements Using Poetry © 2014 by Paul B. Janeczko • Scholastic Teaching Resources

"Quilt"

Janet S. Wong

Our family
is a quilt

of odd remnants
patched together

in a strange
pattern,

threads fraying
fabric wearing thin—

but made to keep
its warmth

even in bitter
cold.

could have them form a chain by holding hands. Although the arrangement sounds simple, it will take practice to make sure that each performer reads his or her line with precise timing, so there's no gap between the lines and, at the same time, no reader steps on the line of the previous performer.

It would be a nice touch to the performance to hang a quilt or two as a backdrop for the readers.

After Reading

After the oral reading, have students reread the poem to themselves and take note of all the comparisons between the quilt and family that they can find. Actually, the poem is one big comparison and students will more than likely pick up on that fact. Discuss with them the comparisons they found in the poem. Ask them if the comparisons between the narrator's family and a quilt make sense. For example, saying that the quilt is made of "odd remnants" could refer to some of the unusual members of her family. Can the class see why Wong chose this metaphor for her poem?

More Great Poems for Teaching Symbolism

"Circles," Myra Cohn Livingston

"The Poison Tree," William Blake

"Junkyards," Julian Lee Rayford

Teaching Literary Elements Using Poetry © 2014 by Paul B. Janeczko • Scholastic Teaching Resources

Writing Activity

Give students a copy of the **Organizer: Family** activity page (page 84). Ask them to fill it out for members of their families. They should jot down thoughts and feelings about the members of their families that they know the best.

Once students have had time to complete the organizer, ask each to think of an object that might symbolize his or her family. Is a family like a precious masterpiece, something that is priceless, something that has endured for a long time? Maybe it is more like a cracked bowl that has been glued back together? When students have chosen suitable symbols, ask each to create a word web with the symbol in the center and the reasons for choosing that symbol on the spokes of the web. Why is that object an apt symbol?

Once students have created family-symbol webs, they can each write a poem about their family, using that symbol as the focal point, or they can each write a short personal essay that describes the object and carefully explains how his or her family is like that object.

Lesson Extensions

* Look for the use of symbolism in other poetry and prose. Make a list of the symbols and their respective meanings.

* Make a drawing of an original symbol, such as a flag, seal, or logo that expresses who you are.

Metaphor

"Mary Todd Lincoln Speaks of Her Son's Death, 1862"
Paul B. Janeczko

Introducing the Literary Element

Metaphor is a direct comparison of two dissimilar things (without using *like* or *as*).

We all use metaphors in our everyday speech. For example, if a person doesn't take care of his personal appearance and can't be bothered to clean his room, we might say, "He's a pig." A major league pitcher who is strong and capable of pitching a lot of innings is often called "a horse." Both of these comparisons are metaphors. And metaphors are common, on television, in movies, and in conversations.

Of course, metaphors abound in literature. Distribute the **Metaphor Examples** activity page (page 85). Read the metaphors aloud. Ask students to explain the connection between the things that are being compared.

When you think students have an understanding of metaphor, you can have them break into groups of two or three. Their task is to brainstorm metaphors they have used themselves or have heard others use, either in the media, in their neighborhoods, or at school. Give the groups enough time to discuss their comparisons and come up with five to

Teaching Literary Elements Using Poetry © 2014 by Paul B. Janeczko • Scholastic Teaching Resources

six metaphors. Make sure that each group is prepared to explain any metaphors that might not be obvious to the class.

After they have had time to create their lists, ask each group to report to the class. Write their responses on the board. When you have filled the board with students' metaphors, ask them to assign the comparisons to a category or an arena where the metaphor might be used. For example, "sports," "neighborhood," "places." When you've put most of the metaphors into categories, and thus shown how metaphors can be about many things, ask the class to supply more metaphors. You can also ask them to come up with metaphors for categories not on the board.

If you notice metaphors that are trite or cliché, this would be a good time to discuss them with the class. For example, talking about a strong mother, a student may have said something like, "She's a rock." That particular comparison, even though it may be apt, has been used so many times that it's lost its originality and impact. It has become a cliché. Although clichés in everyday speech happen all the time, remind students that clichés don't work well in a poem. In other words, a good metaphor for a poem is original and fresh. A good metaphor is also universal, something that readers will understand.

Introducing the Poem

While Abraham Lincoln is one of our country's more revered and popular presidents, students may not be familiar with his wife, Mary Todd Lincoln, or their children. So I decided to write a poem about the death of the Lincoln's middle son as seen through the eyes and heart of Mrs. Lincoln.

My poem is based on the fact that the Lincolns' son, Willie, died of a typhoid-like disease in 1862, a couple of months after his eleventh birthday. More than likely, he contracted the disease from contaminated water that ran in a canal where the president's children played. It was a devastating blow to Lincoln and one of many blows ultimately experienced by his wife.

Mary Todd Lincoln was plagued with insecurities that led to bizarre behavior, like buying 400 pairs of gloves over a four-month period. Her extravagances were the fodder of much gossip, as she fell deeper into debt. In fact, such continued carelessness led her only surviving son, Robert, to commit her to an insane asylum in 1875. She won her own release and died in 1882.

Teaching Literary Elements Using Poetry © 2014 by Paul B. Janeczko • Scholastic Teaching Resources

⋟ Vocabulary ⋞

You might want to point out that *gag* is one of those English words that can be used as different parts of speech. I use it as a verb in "poison that would not kill/only gag me with its bitterness." But, of course, *gag* can also be used as a noun, something placed in or over your mouth to keep you from speaking. And, don't forget that *gag*—in this case a noun—is also a joke or a prank.

Why not spend some time asking your class to supply other English words that can be used as different parts of speech? They might offer words such as *oil*, *part*, *well*, and *run*.

Reading the Poem

Since the narrator of this poem is a woman, it should be read aloud primarily by a girl. But that doesn't mean it's a one-girl poem. President Lincoln has a couple of lines in the first and last stanzas, which a boy could read aloud. I also like the idea of having another reader—or even a small chorus—read the word *Gone* that begins stanzas 2, 3, and 4 for dramatic effect.

Practice is the key to any good oral reading, but especially so when there are a few transitions from one reader (or chorus) to another and back again that must be smoothly handled.

After Reading

After students have had the opportunity to hear the poem performed and have reread it themselves, ask them to identify the three metaphors in the poem by filling out the **Organizer: Metaphor** activity page (page 86). Students need to fill in the boxes with the two things that are being compared and then write a brief explanation of why the two things are compared. They should recognize that the three metaphors I use in the poem are "thunder clap/deafening me," a "curtain/coming down on 11 years," and

Teaching Literary Elements Using Poetry © 2014 by Paul B. Janeczko • Scholastic Teaching Resources

"Mary Todd Lincoln Speaks of Her Son's Death, 1862"

Paul B. Janeczko

When Willie died of the fever
Abraham spoke the words
that I could not:
"My boy is gone.
He is actually gone."

Gone.
The word was a thunder clap
deafening me to my wails
as I folded over his body
already growing cold.

Gone.
The word was a curtain
coming down on 11 years,
hiding toy soldiers,
circus animals,
and his beloved train.

Gone.
The word was poison
but poison that would not kill
only gag me with its bitterness
as I choked on a prayer for my death.

Abraham spoke the words
that I could not:
"My boy is gone.
He is actually gone."
And I am left
with grief that
when spoken
shatters like my heart.

Teaching Literary Elements Using Poetry © 2014 by Paul B. Janeczko • Scholastic Teaching Resources

"poison/but poison that would not kill."

Once students have had time to fill out the organizer, you can project a version and fill it in with the information the class gives you. When you have the class version of the organizer filled in, have students talk about the comparisons and explain if/how the metaphors work for them. Can they see how the metaphors show the way Mary Todd Lincoln feels when she is reminded of her young son's death with the word *Gone*?

More Great Poems for Teaching Metaphor

"Apple," Nan Fry

"Cloud Shadow," Lilian Moore

"Rags," Judith Thurman

Writing Activity

Ask students to read through some of the drafts of the poetry or prose they've turned in from earlier lessons. Have them look for places they could add a metaphor or two to make their writing more expressive. Can they find spots where they can use metaphors as better ways of describing something or someone? Make sure they understand that they are not to change something just for the sake of changing it. Rather, they are making changes or revisions, with a metaphor that will make their prose or poetry better.

If they have no older work they want to reconsider, ask them to write a short descriptive piece that contains a metaphor or two.

Lesson Extensions

- Take part in a week-long Metaphor Alert. Look for metaphors that occur in everyday life, outside of class. Write examples on index cards and post them in the classroom on a Wall of Metaphors.

- Search online for examples of metaphors. Choose 10–12 metaphors and work with a partner to determine what each metaphor means. For example, *Jamal was a library of information* compares the boy's knowledge to the wealth of information found in a library.

Teaching Literary Elements Using Poetry © 2014 by Paul B. Janeczko • Scholastic Teaching Resources

Simile

"Concrete Mixers"
Patricia Hubbell

Introducing the Literary Element

Simile is a comparison using *like* or *as*.

The simile is the first cousin of the metaphor. We find them all over the place in poems. We also find them in our conversations. And, like a metaphor, a simile must have a universal quality. In other words, the reader must be able to understand the comparison. However, as discussed in the previous lesson about metaphors, many similes we hear and use, such as *This is light as a feather* and *He's sick as a dog* are clichés. So, students should resist the temptation to use similes that are clichés and be on the lookout for fresh similes in the poems they read and write.

Have students work in groups of three or four. Each group will have two tasks to complete. The first task is to come up with four to six similes. They can be original similes or ones that students have read or heard in the media. Once they complete their lists, ask each group to read their similes to the class. After each group reports, ask the class if anybody heard any stale comparisons. You might make two columns on the board: one for clichés and one for fresh similes. The class can also judge if there are any similes that are difficult to understand.

The second task for the groups is to write ten fresh similes. They can come up with their own, or they can get some help from the **Simile Starters** activity page (page 87), which includes some starter phrases, such as

- The whale was as large as _____.

- She is as strong as _____.

Encourage each group to be original and fresh with its similes, but not to be so far out that they can't be understood.

Once students have had the chance to work with their groups, you can read one of the prompt lines from the organizer and invite students who have completed that simile to read it to the class. For each set of responses to the prompt, ask the class to vote on the most successful similes.

Introducing the Poem

Since Patricia Hubbell's poem builds on the comparison of concrete mixers and elephants, it might help to show students pictures of both. You could search the Internet for images (or scan some you may already have) and create a slide show to introduce the poem, which could be used later as a backdrop for a performance of the poem.

Once students have had a chance to see some images of elephants and concrete mixers, discuss the differences. Then discuss the similarities and invite students to pay close attention to the poet's references to each while reading "Concrete Mixers."

⇒ Vocabulary ⇐

Here are some words and phrases students may not know: *elephant tenders* (not something you find in a fast food restaurant), *ponderous*, *perch* (another word that works as different parts of speech), *mahouts*, *trough*, *bulging*, *bellow*, *urban*.

Reading the Poem

As mentioned above, a slide show of elephants and concrete mixers could be used as a backdrop for a performance of this poem. Students could refine the slide show with photos of elephants doing some of the things that are happening to the concrete mixers.

You could have a single student read aloud the poem, but I'd like to suggest something that involves more students. How about breaking it into parts: four readers for the first 11 lines, another reader for the four short lines, and a sixth reader for the final two lines.

Since there is action described in the poem, you might try having students act out some of the actions, almost like a slow-motion ballet!

Teaching Literary Elements Using Poetry © 2014 by Paul B. Janeczko • Scholastic Teaching Resources

"Concrete Mixers"
Patricia Hubbell

The drivers are washing the concrete mixers;
Like elephant tenders they hose them down.
Tough grey-skinned monsters standing ponderous,
Elephant-bellied and elephant-nosed,
Standing in muck up to their wheel-caps,
Like rows of elephants, tail to trunk.
Their drivers perch on their backs like mahouts,
Sending the sprays of water up.
They rid the trunk-like trough of concrete,
Direct the spray to the bulging sides,
Turn and start the monsters moving.
    Concrete mixers
    Move like elephants
    Bellow like elephants
    Spray like elephants,
Concrete mixers are urban elephants,
Their trunks are raising a city.

Teaching Literary Elements Using Poetry © 2014 by Paul B. Janeczko • Scholastic Teaching Resources

After Reading

Ask students to reread "Concrete Mixers" and take note wherever *like* appears in the poem. They will find the word used seven times; and six of which indicate a simile. Your class might recognize that each simile is associated with an action. For example, the first two lines of the poem: "The drivers are washing the concrete mixers;/ Like elephant tenders they hose them down." Give each student a copy of the **Organizer: Simile** activity page (page 88). Ask students to write the similes from the poem in the left-hand column and explain each simile in the right-hand column. What things are being compared?

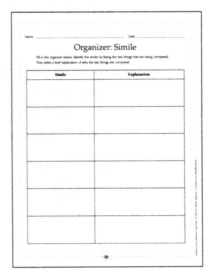

Other comparisons: While similes are the foundation of the poem, Hubbell makes a number of other comparisons between elephants and concrete mixers. For example, "Tough grey-skinned monsters standing ponderous." Ask students to identify these other points of comparison. As they suggest other comparisons, you can write them on the board or chart paper.

More Great Poems for Teaching Simile

"Deserted Farm," Mark Vinz

"Gang," Lois Lenski

"Troubled Woman," Langston Hughes

Teaching Literary Elements Using Poetry © 2014 by Paul B. Janeczko • Scholastic Teaching Resources

Writing Activity

Have students work in pairs. Their task is to create a template for another pair of students to use to come up with similes. The basic model will be a postcard that someone might send to a friend, with sentence starters to be filled in with similes. Once each pair has completed the postcard, the pairs will exchange postcards and fill in the blanks.

Here's an example to show the class:

Greetings from the zoo!
    We have seen lots of interesting animals. The lion's roar was as loud as
_____. You should have seen the giraffe, with a neck as long as _____.
The cheetah moves as fast as _____. Not like the tortoise. His shell is like
_____. The only problem was the bus to the parking lot. We were packed in
like _____.

Tell students that they can add *a/an* before the actual simile. For example, they might say, *His shell is like a/an _____.* The important things for them to remember as they work on this activity:

• Make sure their comparisons help the reader get a better picture of the image they're describing.

• Avoid clichés. Remind students to be fresh and original.

When they are finished, students may read their postcards to the class. You might also have them illustrate the postcards. Can't you imagine large picture postcards with great similes adorning the walls of your classroom?

Lesson Extensions

Look for similes in other poems and prose and keep a list of them.

Make a Venn diagram comparing elephants and concrete mixers. Refer to the poem and/or find more facts about each to include.

Teaching Literary Elements Using Poetry © 2014 by Paul B. Janeczko • Scholastic Teaching Resources

Personification

"Crumble!"
Lisa Westberg Peters

Introducing the Literary Element

Personification is giving human qualities to inanimate objects.

Poets are always looking for ways to "power up" their poems. By that I mean using language in ways that make the poem come alive for readers. Sometimes a poet will do that with her word choice. For example, rather than describe something as simply red, she may choose to describe it as *scarlet*, *vermillion*, *crimson*, *ruby*, *cherry*, *cardinal*, or *rose*. Poets also bring their poems to life when they compare one thing to another, perhaps with a metaphor or simile. They can also do it with personification. But like using metaphor and simile, it is easy to fall into using personification in an exaggerated way, which is called *pathetic fallacy*. Students need not know that term, but they should know to tread carefully when they use personification. A stanza from Alfred Lord Tennyson's "Maud" is a frequent example of pathetic fallacy:

There has fallen a splendid tear
      From the passion-flower at the gate.
She is coming, my dove, my dear;
      She is coming, my life, my fate.
The red rose cries, "She is near, she is near;"
      And the white rose weeps, "She is late;"
The larkspur listens, "I hear, I hear;"
      And the lily whispers, "I wait."

Teaching Literary Elements Using Poetry © 2014 by Paul B. Janeczko • Scholastic Teaching Resources

Of course, not only poets are guilty of using such excess. Here's an example from *Jane Eyre*: "Nature must be gladsome when I was so happy." Advertising is one of the worst offenders, such as this slogan for the city of Philadelphia: "The City That Loves You Back." Well, a city cannot "love you back," any more than nature can be glad when you are happy.

Distribute copies of the **Organizer: Personification** activity page (page 89). Then show students effective examples of personification in various texts. Have students record these examples on the organizer to keep for reference.

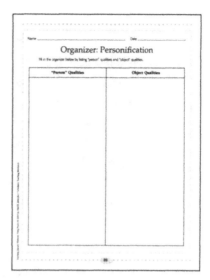

Introducing the Poem

"Crumble!" comes from a wonderful Lisa Westberg Peters' collection called *Earthshake: Poems From the Ground Up*—a fine example of poems that can be used across the curriculum. In addition to poems about such things as glaciers, quartz, lava, and the earth's plates, Peters includes in her collection three pages of endnotes that further explore the scientific principals that she brings to life in her poems.

Peters uses personification in a couple of ways in "Crumble!" By writing a poem of address (a poem written to an inanimate object), she gives to sandstone the human qualities of being able to hear. In fact, she begins the poem by addressing sandstone directly, "Sandstone, you have one response to life." Beyond that, she refers to sandstone's "grandpa" and "grandma," who have "passed on to you/their memories." The poet also personifies the wind by writing, "The wind says hello." The poem avoids pathetic fallacy because we recognize that Peters is speaking metaphorically.

≽ Vocabulary ≼

There are a few geological terms in this poem that students may not know: *lagoon, dune, delta, sandbar, squall.*

Students will no doubt notice that, in addition to being the title of the poem, *crumble* is repeated four times in the poem. And each time it is used in the poem, it's part of an exclamation, "You crumble!" Such repetition serves a couple of purposes in the poem. It ties the poem together, from its title to its last word. In addition, that phrase emphasizes one of the points that Peters is writing about: the fragility of sandstone.

Reading the Poem

The narrator of "Crumble!" addresses sandstone directly. Although there is a single narrator, it might be interesting to have multiple students read the lines aloud, which may emphasize the scolding tone of the narrator. You might divide the opening lines of the poem in this way: Reader 1: lines 1–3; Reader 2: lines 4–5; Reader 3: lines 6–7. For the rest of the poem, you could try having different students read one sentence each.

Can you think of another way to present this poem? You might choose to have one student read the whole poem, except "You crumble!" That phrase could be read by a small chorus or even the entire class.

Teaching Literary Elements Using Poetry © 2014 by Paul B. Janeczko • Scholastic Teaching Resources

"Crumble!"
Lisa Westberg Peters

Sandstone,
you have one response to life.
You crumble!
A foot falls on you.
You crumble!
The wind says hello.
You crumble!

Remember your noble past.
Your grandpa was a lagoon.
Your grandma, a dune.
You come from a long line
of deltas and sandbars.
They've passed on to you
their memories of sudden squalls
and sea monsters.
Toughen up, sandstone.

But you don't.
You crumble!

After Reading

Once students have reread "Crumble!" and you have had a chance to discuss the elements of personification in it, break the class into groups of two or three and give each group the Personification organizer to fill out. Point out that students should focus on the qualities of sandstone. In the left-hand column, students will write about the "person" of sandstone. In the right-hand column they will write about the physical qualities it posses as a sedimentary rock. Make sure everything that students note can be verified in the poem.

> ### *More Great Poems for Teaching Personification*
>
> "Timber Rattlesnake," Marilyn Singer
>
> "Vacuum Cleaner's Revenge," Patricia Hubbell
>
> "The Cow's Complaint," Alice Schertle

Writing Activity

After students have had time to read and explore "Crumble!," have them try their hand at writing a poem of address that also includes several examples of personification.

Before students begin looking for ideas for their poems, I recommend that you give them two or three other poems of address with personification to read.

Once students have completed the poems, encourage them to augment their work with drawings, photographs, or sketches. Then compile students' poems into an anthology.

Lesson Extensions

- Although the properties of sandstone may be apparent from its name, conduct research at the library or online to find out a bit more about this rock. Write a brief essay about what you learned.

- Rewrite "Crumble!" from the point of view of the sandstone. How is the personification of sandstone the same or different from the original poem?

Teaching Literary Elements Using Poetry © 2014 by Paul B. Janeczko • Scholastic Teaching Resources

Alliteration

"Toby Twits Tina"
Jeanne Steig

Introducing the Literary Element

Alliteration is the repetition of initial consonant sounds.

Why use alliteration in poetry? Poetry is, among other things, sound. Poems are often meant to be read aloud because listening is an effective way for a reader to grasp the full intent of the poet. Alliteration is a sound-focused literary device.

Alliteration is not hard for students to recognize. They hear examples of alliteration all day—if they pay attention. There are examples in advertisements and business names. Many celebrities even have alliterative names.

Distribute copies of the **Organizer: Alliteration** activity page (page 90) and give students time to fill in some examples of alliteration that they encounter in everyday life—when they shop in stores, read magazines, and watch TV or movies.

Students are also familiar with tongue twisters, another source of enjoyable alliteration, such as the classic *Peter Piper picked a peck of pickled peppers.* Can they suggest other tongue twister? Here are a few you can recite as examples:

- *Timmy tricked Teddy and took his train off the track.*

- *On Monday Mona's mother Mary mostly mopped.*

Teaching Literary Elements Using Poetry © 2014 by Paul B. Janeczko • Scholastic Teaching Resources

• *John got juice and jam on his jade jacket when Judy jumped on him.*

• *Ruth and Rachel ran after Richard's rotund rabbit.*

I suspect that students will have fun swapping tongue twisters they've heard.

Introducing the Poem

Once you have introduced the notion of alliteration, project "Toby Twits Tina" on the board and use a bright color to highlight the use of *t* in the poem. Students will immediately see the many words that start with *t*. Remind them to keep an ear out for the *t* sound when they listen to the poem—that it can fall within a word, not just at the beginning—and to think about how alliteration can be an effective literary device.

⇒ Vocabulary ⇐

This playful poem includes a number of words that students may not know: *semolina, tactful, throttle, torment, tapioca*. And don't forget *twits* in the title!

This is a good chance to remind students how English words can work as different parts of speech. Have them explore how *throttle* and *torment* can be used as a noun as well as a verb, as they are used in this poem. Can they come up with any other words in the poem that can be different parts of speech? *Taunt* and *tweak*, for example, can also serve as nouns and verbs.

Reading the Poem

Once you have highlighted all the alliterative words, ask a few students to read the poem aloud so everyone can hear the alliteration. The poem is written in eight lines, and since each captures something of a complete thought, a different student could read each line.

Point out that "Toby Twits Tina" calls for more careful enunciation than usual to ensure that listeners hear the alliteration and catch the humor in Jeanne Steig's poem.

An alternative approach is to have a small group read the poem as a formal and somewhat "upper crust" recitation.

Teaching Literary Elements Using Poetry © 2014 by Paul B. Janeczko • Scholastic Teaching Resources

"Toby Twits Tina"

Jeanne Steig

Toby's teasing can be tasteless
Taunting, tweaking tiny Tina.
Tadpoles in her tapioca!
Thumbtacks in her semolina!

Toby ought to be more tactful.
If he's tempted to torment her,
Let him tickle, never throttle,
Never thump her, lest he dent her.

Teaching Literary Elements Using Poetry © 2014 by Paul B. Janeczko • Scholastic Teaching Resources

After Reading

Ask students to reread the poem and focus again on each example of alliteration. As a class, discuss the effectiveness of alliteration in "Toby Twits Tina." Does it make the poem more interesting or memorable? Does it distract the reader from thinking about how mean Toby is really acting?

More Great Poems for Teaching Alliteration

"For You," Karla Kuskin

"Building," Gwendolyn Brooks

"Street Painter," Ann Turner

Writing Activity

Have students try their hand at writing their own version of an alliterative poem. Invite students to work in pairs. Each pair will need to come up with at least four lines that mimic Steig's first stanza. They need to decide which consonant they will emphasize in their poem. Allow the pairs some wiggle room regarding how strictly they need to follow Steig, but encourage them to stick to her model as closely as possible. You might suggest these lines as an example of what their poems should sound like:

> Ronald's ribbing can be repulsive
> Ridiculing, rejecting rigid Richard.
> Red pepper in his raisins!
> Roaches in his rice!

You may want to give the writing pairs time to write an eight-line poem as Steig did. This activity works best if students have access to dictionaries and thesauruses.

Lesson Extensions

※ Bring in a poem that is more effective when read aloud. Jack Prelutsky and Shel Silverstein have written plenty, but consider some of the classic American poets. Be prepared to read the poem to the class.

※ Write a mini Alliteration Anthology. Pick any subject, such as friendship, animals, or transportation. Write five original tongue twisters that have to do with that subject.

Teaching Literary Elements Using Poetry © 2014 by Paul B. Janeczko • Scholastic Teaching Resources

Onomatopoeia

"Washing Machine"
Bobbi Katz

Introducing the Literary Element

Onomatopoeia refers to the use of words that sound like the objects they name or the sounds these objects make, like *tick-tock*, *quack*, *moo*, and *buzz*.

Although this literary term may be one of the most difficult to spell, it is one of the easiest to understand. It comes from the Greek words, which approximate *I make a name* or *making of a name*. I'd prefer that it be called something like "noise word." While some poems have a noise word or two in them, "Washing Machine" is a delightful smorgasbord of such words. Whatever you call these words, students can have a ball with them.

Divide students into teams of three. Distribute copies of the **Organizer: Onomatopoeia** activity page (page 91). Each group must come up with as many examples of onomatopoeia as it can in a limited amount of time, say 10 to 15 minutes, and write them in the Word column of the organizer. They should also name something that might make that sound. When time has expired, have one team member from each group read the words, but read them as quickly as he or she can. It's important for students to hear the sound of these noise words. Following the speedy recitation, have the student read the words again, this time slowly enough so you can write them on the board or chart paper, eliminating duplicates each group reports. When the list is final, it's time for a choral recitation by the class. Try different approaches to see if variations affect how the words sound. For example, you could have all the girls read, then all the boys. You can read the list quickly, then at normal speed.

Following the recitation, send students back to their teams. Their task this time is to study the entire list that the class came up with, then come up with eight to ten words that have something in common in addition to being onomatopoeia. It could be words that have the short-*i* sound, such as *blip* and *click*. Or a list can include sounds from nature, such *roar* and *buzz*. Once the students have created their lists, it's time for another recitation. Have some fun with these fun words!

Introducing the Poem

"Washing Machine" is a *persona poem*, which many people call a *mask poem* because the poet is, in a sense, wearing a mask as she pretends to be the object that is speaking in the poem. The first line of the poem should tell students that this is a persona poem: *I'm the washing machine*. The second line builds on that: *I make dirty clothes clean*. As students read the rest of the poem, they will see the pronoun *I* used throughout, right up to the final line, *I stop*.

One of the highlights of this poem is its use of onomatopoeia. Just like a typical washing machine, this poem has a lot of sounds to share!

≫ Vocabulary ≪

There are no difficult "real" words in this poem, but other delightful "sound words" might challenge some of your less able readers, such as *glubita*, *glub*, *swizzle-dee-swash*, and *Babba-da-swaba*. But, if you break these words into syllables and recite them aloud, most students will take to them with little trouble.

Reading the Poem

Bobbi Katz uses a number of nonsense words in this poem, but they become less intimidating and more fun when they are read aloud. In fact, her poem is a perfect poem to read aloud.

One way to approach performing this poem is to divide it into two parts. One person or group can read the "regular" words that the washing machine says. For example: "I'm the washing machine./I make dirty clothes clean,/so that nobody has to rub:"

Teaching Literary Elements Using Poetry © 2014 by Paul B. Janeczko • Scholastic Teaching Resources

"Washing Machine"

Bobbi Katz

I'm the washing machine.
I make dirty clothes clean,
so that nobody has to rub:

Glubita glubita glubita
Glubita glubita glubita . . .
GLUB.
Swizzle-dee-swash—
Swizzle-dee-swash—

I talk to myself,
while I do the wash!

Babba-da-swaba—

I change my song
as the cycle moves along.
Soapsuds gurgle through my hose.
Then . . .

Blub-blub-a-dubba—

I rinse the clothes.

Blippety-blop—
Blippety-blop—
I spin, spin, spin

and then . . .
I stop.

Teaching Literary Elements Using Poetry © 2014 by Paul B. Janeczko • Scholastic Teaching Resources

Another person or group reads the sounds that the washing machine makes—these "words" sound better coming from a group—like *Glubita* and *Swizzle-dee-swash*.

Invite students to suggest ways to make this poem come alive on the stage. I bet they could come up with great ideas.

After Reading

Amid the onomatopoeia in "Washing Machine," Katz has created a mask poem. By its nature, a mask poem is a poem of personification, since the poet is giving human qualities to an inanimate object. Of particular importance is the ability of the object to speak. Give students a copy of the **Organizer: Mask Poem** activity page (page 92), which asks them to list all the things the washing-machine claims to do. Most of the things it does are normal washing-machine duties. But there are two spots where the washing machine is speaking metaphorically. Ask your students to mark those two things on their lists.

More Great Poems for Teaching Onomatopoeia

"Broom," Tony Johnston

"Laughing Child," Carl Sandburg

"Onomatopoeia," Eve Merriam

Teaching Literary Elements Using Poetry © 2014 by Paul B. Janeczko • Scholastic Teaching Resources

Writing Activity

Now that students have spent time examining sound words and considering what makes a mask poem, it's time for them to use what they've learned to create mask poems of their own, using "Washing Machine" as a model.

There are a couple of ways they can approach the assignment. They might begin by looking over the examples of onomatopoeia they generated with their groups and take note of what might make that sound, filling in column 2 of their organizers. They can also think about the onomatopoetic words the class generated, especially the work they did finding related words, for instance, words from nature. As they look at their lists, they might see that many of the sounds are related to birds, let's say, or machines. Each student can go from there and begin brainstorming with a writing partner about what to include in the poem.

Some students might prefer to choose a subject and then try to generate some sound words that are associated with it. For instance, they might choose sound words that are related to cars or trucks.

As they work on their poems, remind students that they need not load the poem with every conceivable sound word. They should only include those that are best suited to the poem. Remind them also that they are each writing a complete poem, not just a list of neat-sounding words. This means that they should build their poems with only the most appropriate words to create an image that readers will recognize.

Lesson Extensions

❋ Look in other literature for onomatopoeia like the words created by Katz in her poem. Write examples on index cards and post them in the classroom on a Wall of Onomatopoeia. Be sure to include the name of the story or poem in which you found the example, as well as its author, on each card you contribute.

❋ Make up your own onomatopoetic words for a washing machine and substitute them in Katz's poem.

Mood

"Junkyard Dog"
Tony Johnston

Introducing the Literary Element

Mood is the atmosphere or general feeling in a work of literature.

Students understand that a mood is the way they feel at a particular time. In reply to someone asking, "How are you?" a student might say he is happy, sad, frustrated, or relaxed. In a poem, mood is the feeling that the poet creates. In "Junkyard Dog," Tony Johnston creates a mood of lurking danger.

Ask students to suggest specific parts of movies and TV shows that create a mood. They might mention some of the hair-raising scenes in the Harry Potter or Twilight movies. Ask students what helps create that mood. Is it character? The setting of a scene? The background music?

You can continue this discussion by asking students the same questions about a novel or short story they may have read in your class. Perhaps there are scenes in the current novel your class is reading that can be included in this discussion about mood.

To make sure students understand that moods can be as varied as works of literature, be certain that this discussion includes moods other than scary or creepy. For instance, a certain poem or song might create a peaceful or joyful mood. Movies do the same thing.

Teaching Literary Elements Using Poetry © 2014 by Paul B. Janeczko • Scholastic Teaching Resources

Introducing the Poem

Point out that "Junkyard Dog," contains many words that evoke a particular mood. When students read the poem, have them take note of these words and think about how the words contribute to the overall mood Johnston is trying to achieve. In addition to choosing words that evoke a mood in the poem, the poet also skillfully uses rhyme and alliteration. On the first or subsequent readings, you can also invite students to find examples of the repetition of the *r* sound early in the poem, as occur in *wreck, rust, rules, ruined.* (Remind them that alliteration is about *sound* not spelling, so *wreck* is alliterative with the other words I mentioned, even though the others start with *r*.) While these words do not immediately follow one another, they are close enough to be considered alliteration. Johnston also uses alliteration with *disdained/domain,* and late in the poem with *gravel/growl.*

⇒ Vocabulary ⇐

Students may not know the meaning of these words: *disdained, domain, slinking, mangy.*

The rhyming words in this poem may not be obvious to students because Johnston doesn't rhyme words at the end of lines, where we would normally expect to find it. Rather she rhymes in the middle of lines, with word pairs like *mangled/tangled* and *domain/chain.*

Reading the Poem

How can students read this poem in a way that captures its mood? Performing it on a dimly lit stage might help. Perhaps a simple set of a fence would be a nice touch. As far as reading the poem itself, I see it as a kind of rap, with a staccato and harsh delivery. The reader might even perform the poem with "the gravel of a growl."

Ask a couple students to read "Junkyard Dog." Choose different voices for your first readings and make sure the class hears the poem read by boys and girls.

If you'd like to involve more students, you can create a "junkyard chorus" of six students, with each reading one sentence of the poem. Such an arrangement may not sound very complicated, however students will need to practice their parts thoroughly to make sure they begin their sentence precisely and not allow a gap between the end of one sentence and the beginning of the next.

Although the movie *West Side Story* may seem dated for your students, you might want to show them a couple of scenes where the Sharks and the Jets deliver their finger-snapping lines.

Teaching Literary Elements Using Poetry © 2014 by Paul B. Janeczko • Scholastic Teaching Resources

"Junkyard Dog"

Tony Johnston

Watch thou and wake
when others be asleep.
 — William Shakespeare

In the metal forest of scrap
and hubcap, wreck and rust,
                    he rules,
guardian of the ruined,
the mangled, the tangled,
the disdained.
His domain is measured in the links
of a chain.
No slinking for him.
He is the king
          of lunge
and fang.
When he dozes on his mangy
heap,
the gravel of a growl
sticks in his throat.
Beware his fearful shape,
watchful even in sleep!

Teaching Literary Elements Using Poetry © 2014 by Paul B. Janeczko • Scholastic Teaching Resources

After Reading

After the reading, ask students how they felt as they heard the poem. Could they describe in a word or two the mood that the poem creates? Write their responses on the board. Give the class time to share thoughts on the mood of the poem. Ask students to read "Junkyard Dog" to themselves, and take note of all the words in the poem that contribute to evoking the mood described by the words you've written on the board. The poem's words and phrases they circle will include some of these: *scrap, wreck, rust, ruined, tangled, mangled, slinking, lunge and fang, mangy heap, gravel of a growl, beware, fearful.*

Most of the words, of course, describe the dog. Beyond the first few lines of the poem—"In the metal forest of scrap/and hubcap, wreck and rust"—we don't get any description of the junkyard. So, it is clearly the description of the dog that creates the mood/atmosphere of menace and fear.

More Great Poems for Teaching Mood

"The Raven," Edgar Allan Poe

'Whispers to the Wall," Rebecca Kai Dotlich

"Tugboats at Daybreak," Lillian Morrison

Writing Activity

Distribute the **Organizer: Mood** activity page (page 93) to each student. The organizer has space for students to choose various moods and then list below them words that they feel might create that mood. For example, they might choose *sad* as a mood and list words like: *gloom, dreary, cheerless, dismal, grim.* You can allow students to use a thesaurus on this activity, but I would suggest you resist doing so until they have had time to compile a list based on the contributions of all the members of their groups.

Teaching Literary Elements Using Poetry © 2014 by Paul B. Janeczko • Scholastic Teaching Resources

Students can refer to their organizers for help in writing each own's mood piece. Each may write a personal narrative that tells of a real-life experience that was frightening, for instance, or made the student off-the-charts happy. Or, each may write a poem or short piece of fiction that expresses a specific mood. Make sure they understand that they need not imitate the mood created in "Junkyard Dog" or in any of the scary movies they brought up in the class discussion. As students work on brainstorming, drafting, and revising, ask each to circle the words that create the desired mood to help identify the impact of certain words and phrases in the piece.

Lesson Extensions

- Play a word game with a partner or small group. The first person chooses a word that describes an emotion. Then, take turns naming different synonyms for the word. See how many words you can come up with.

- Go to an Internet thesaurus and find synonyms for some mood words, such as *gloomy*, *joyous*, *quiet*, *tense*, and *silly*. You can also come up with your own mood words to check out in a thesaurus.

Teaching Literary Elements Using Poetry © 2014 by Paul B. Janeczko • Scholastic Teaching Resources

Poetic Patterns

"Riding the Wind"
Doris Bircham

Introducing the Literary Element

Poetic patterns are structural repetition found most often in rhyming poems.

Rhyming poems follow a pattern. There are a number of poetic elements that can be part of the pattern, but rhyme and rhythm top the list. It is repetition that make rhyming poems so popular with young readers. No doubt many students are fans of Jack Prelutsky and Shel Silverstein. Yes, they are frequently hilarious, but kids also respond to the sound and bounce of their poems. In addition to repetitions in rhythm and rhyme, stanza form is also part of the pattern.

Distribute copies of the **Organizer: Poetic Patterns** activity page (page 94), which includes four common categories of patterns used in poetry. Discuss elements of each one with students.

- Sound—students should consider the rhythm and rhyme

- Repetition—students should consider specific words and phrases that are repeated

- Stanza—students should consider the number of lines in each stanza and their rhyme scheme

- Length of line—students should consider the number of syllables and any stressed syllables in the different lines

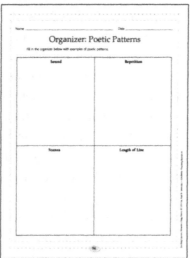

Let students know that they will fill in this graphic organizer specifically after reading the next poem, but that they can use copies of this organizer to help them identify patterns in other poems they read.

Introducing the Poem

"Riding the Wind" is a lively poem that features several examples of poetic patterns. Its author, Doris Bircham, is considered a "cowboy poet," a group of men and women who earn their livelihood working cattle ranches in the western part of the United States. These poets write mostly traditional rhyming poems—like Bircham's—about life "home on the range." The vocabulary she uses is also part of the pattern of this poem.

⇒ Vocabulary ⇐

Several words will likely be unfamiliar to students: *chinook, nook, loping*. In addition to those words, Bircham uses vocabulary related to horses as she speaks metaphorically of her journey. Point out the "horse words" to students: *loping, saddled, reins, spur, whinny, mount up, jump on its back*.

Reading the Poem

Begin the lesson by reading "Riding the Wind" once aloud in a timid, halting voice, so students will notice the different impact of a more exuberant delivery. Then ask a couple of students—boys and girls—to read the poem aloud so the class can hear the rhythms and rhymes in the poem. It's a rousing poem, so try to select at least one student who can give the poem its due in that regard. The poem does need to gallop along, and hearing a contrast in reading styles might make that decision about pacing more evident to your class.

As I mentioned above, this is a lively poem. The poet is, after all, imagining "Riding the Wind." How best to capture that in a performance? I see this work as a choral piece, perhaps with different groups of students reading each stanza. Because the first line of each stanza serves as a refrain (a group of words repeated in a poem or song), you might assign a different group or an individual student to read that line, as well as the second line that completes its sentence. The rest of the chorus will recite the next three lines.

Don't be afraid to experiment with performance strategies. Different styles suit different readers, so find out what works best with each particular class.

Teaching Literary Elements Using Poetry © 2014 by Paul B. Janeczko • Scholastic Teaching Resources

"Riding the Wind"

Doris Bircham

I am going to ride the wind
when it's blowing hard and strong.
I'll jump on its back
and we'll follow a track
where clouds go loping along.

I am going to ride the wind
when it chases behind the rain,
and whenever it snows
I'll be saddled to go
I'll mount up and grab hold of the reins.

I am going to ride the wind
when it turns to a warm Chinook.
We'll spur to the moon,
whistle springtime tunes
and melt icicles in every nook.

I am going to ride the wind
when it whispers to waving grass.
We'll call out to the creek,
sing flowers to sleep
and whinny "Good Night" as we pass.

After Reading

Once students have heard the poem, ask each to read it again and use the Patterns organizer to record everything that seems to be part of a pattern. Remind them that in this case the point of the organizer is to help categorize elements that can be part of the pattern in a rhyming poem.

Give students a chance to fill in their organizers, then have a class discussion and invite students to share what they noticed. Project a copy of the organizer on the board and, as students mention possible patterns, you could write it in the most appropriate category, understanding that there will be overlap from one category to another. For example, *rhyme* is part of a sound pattern, but it is also part of a stanza pattern. Be sure students come away from the discussion noting the use of a refrain.

Working with the organizer should allow students to see that a good rhyming poem is carefully orchestrated with a number of patterns and repetitions. These patterns help make the poem a coherent unit.

You can reinforce what students have learned about pattern poems by choosing one of the poems listed below—or another rhyming poem—and asking students to read through it and fill out a new copy of the **Organizer: Poetic Patterns** activity page.

More Great Poems for Poetic Patterns

"The Underwater Wibbles" Jack Prelutsky

"Who Clogged Up Our Schoolbell with Bubblegum?" X.J. Kennedy

"Remember," Christine Rossetti

Teaching Literary Elements Using Poetry © 2014 by Paul B. Janeczko • Scholastic Teaching Resources

Writing Activity

Rhyming poems are easily parodied, just by imitating the style but changing the words of the original poem. Are your students ready to create a parody of "Riding the Wind"? They need not write a poem as long as this one, but a couple of stanzas is a reasonable expectation. However, if students work in small writing teams of two or three, they may be able to write a longer collaborative poem.

Writing a parody poem teaches structure by requiring students to stick to the same rhythm, rhyme, and line length, which are all key poetic patterns. If tackling a longer poem proves too challenging as a first attempt, you might suggest that students parody nursery rhymes.

In addition, students can try their hands at writing a pattern poem without it being a parody. Encourage students to try writing something more along the lines of a story poem or ballad, such as "The Golden Vanity" or one of the other poems mentioned in Lesson 1. Allowing students to work in small teams is also a good approach for this activity.

If time permits, give students the opportunity to perform their poems, considering the same guidelines that you used for the class performance of "Riding the Wind."

Lesson Extensions

- Find out more about Bircham and other "cowboy poets." Why are they known as cowboy poets"?

- Compare Bircham's poem to a poem by another "cowboy poet." How are they the same and different?

REPRODUCIBLE ACTIVITY PAGES

Name _____   Date _____

Organizer: Plot Boxes

Fill in the organizer below to help summarize a plot. If you notice a cause-effect relationship, draw an arrow from the box showing the cause to the box showing the effect. (Not all of the boxes will need to be linked in this way, and some effects may become causes that lead to another effect.)

1.	2.
3.	4.
5.	6.
7.	8.
9.	10.

Teaching Literary Elements Using Poetry © 2014 by Paul B. Janeczko • Scholastic Teaching Resources

Name _____ Date _____

Organizer: Plot Line

Use this organizer to help you keep track of the events leading up to the plot climax and to record the resolution.

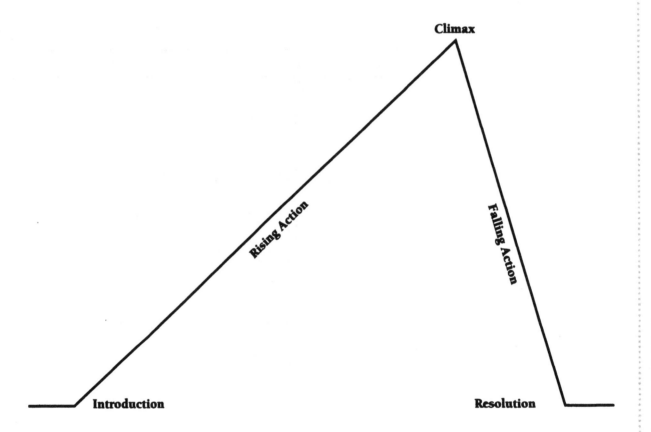

Teaching Literary Elements Using Poetry © 2014 by Paul B. Janeczko • Scholastic Teaching Resources

Mini-Booklet Template

Follow the directions below to create a mini-book.

1. Cut out the figure below along the solid lines.

2. Place the piece labeled "title" on top of the other panel.

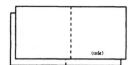

3. Fold along the dotted line. Staple.

4. Number each page in its outer corner. The title page will be first, followed by pages 2, 3, 4, 5, 6, 7, and 8 (the last page).

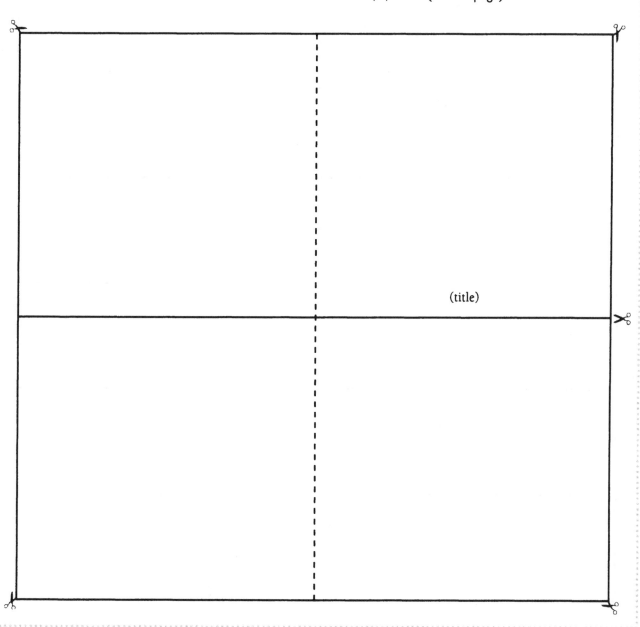

(title)

Organizer: Setting 1

Fill in the organizer below to list setting details from novels you've read or movies you've seen.
Be specific in your descriptions.

Book/Movie	Details of Setting

Organizer: Setting 2

Fill in the organizer below to list setting details from a poem you've read. Be specific in your descriptions.

_____   _____
(Poem)   (Author)

Details of Setting

Teaching Literary Elements Using Poetry © 2014 by Paul B. Janeczko • Scholastic Teaching Resources

Name _____ Date _____

Organizer: Character

In the chart below, record some favorite characters from literature you've read and movies and TV shows you've seen. Think about why these characters are your favorites.

Literature, Movie, TV Show	Favorite Characters

Teaching Literary Elements Using Poetry © 2014 by Paul B. Janeczko • Scholastic Teaching Resources

Name _____   Date _____

Organizer: Character Web

Fill in the boxes at the end of each line with something that *shows* you important aspects of the character.

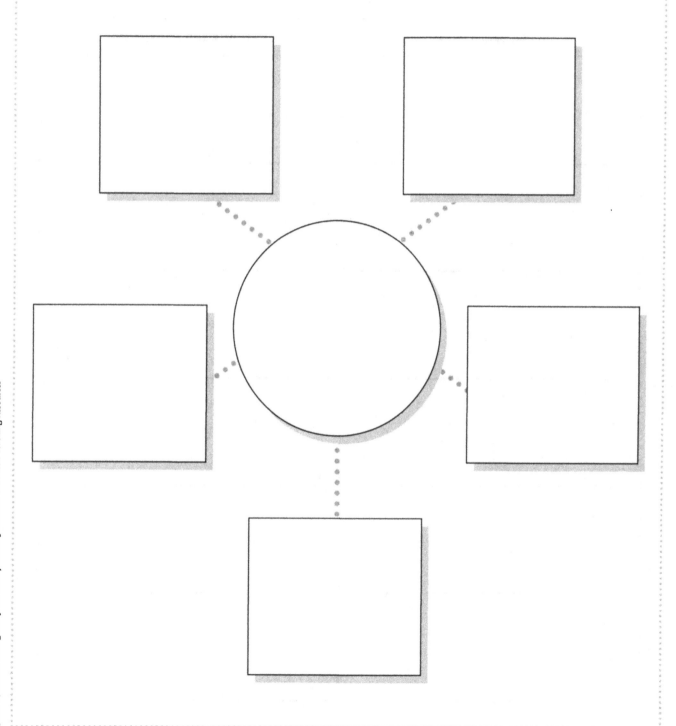

Organizer: Theme

List the titles of some fiction you've read. Then decide the theme of each one.

Novel, Short Story	Explanation of Theme

Teaching Literary Elements Using Poetry © 2014 by Paul B. Janeczko • Scholastic Teaching Resources

Organizer: Symbolism

List six symbols and explain the meaning of each.

Symbol	Explanation

Teaching Literary Elements Using Poetry © 2014 by Paul B. Janeczko • Scholastic Teaching Resources

Organizer: Family

List qualities of some family members you know very well.

Family member: **Qualities:**	**Family member:** **Qualities:**
Family member: **Qualities:**	**Family member:** **Qualities:**
Family member: **Qualities:**	**Family member:** **Qualities:**

Teaching Literary Elements Using Poetry © 2014 by Paul B. Janeczko • Scholastic Teaching Resources

Name _____ Date _____

Metaphor Examples

Read the metaphors below and think about the connection between what is being compared.

1. "The doors of wisdom are never shut."
   Benjamin Franklin, *Poor Richard's Almanack*

2. "Time is the best teacher."
   Anonymous proverb

3. "The bright branches of sheer lightning . . ."
   Pindar, "Pythia 4," *Odes*

4. "The maple wears a gayer scarf,/The field a scarlet gown."
   Emily Dickinson, "Nature, XXVIII, Autumn"

5. "He was a cork that could not be kept under water many moments at a time."
   Mark Twain, *The Gilded Age*

6. "The streets were filled with the rush hour flood of people."
   O. Henry, "An Unfinished Story"

7. "A book is a garden carried in the pocket."
   Arabian proverb

8. "She brushed a cloud of hair out of her eyes . . ."
   John Steinbeck, "The Chrysanthemums"

9. "But the wheat and grass were sleek velvet under the sunset."
   Sinclair Lewis, *Main Street*

10. "His crackers don't sit well in my bowl of soup."
    Bo Jackson (American athlete)

Organizer: Metaphor

Fill in the organizer below. Identify the metaphor by listing the two things that are being compared. Then write a brief explanation of why the two things are compared.

Metaphor	Explanation

Teaching Literary Elements Using Poetry © 2014 by Paul B. Janeczko • Scholastic Teaching Resources

Name _____ Date _____

Simile Starters

Use the starter phrases below to come up with ten fresh similes.

1. The whale was as large as _____ .

2. She is as strong as _____ .

3. His mood was as temperamental as _____ .

4. The celebrity was as sleek as _____ .

5. Her grip was like _____ .

6. The setting sun was like _____ .

7. In the storm, the trees swayed like _____ .

8. When it comes to facts, his brain is like _____ .

9. The icy parking lot is as slippery as _____ .

10. Her voice was like _____ .

Organizer: Simile

Fill in the organizer below. Identify the simile by listing the two things that are being compared. Then write a brief explanation of why the two things are compared.

Simile	Explanation

Teaching Literary Elements Using Poetry © 2014 by Paul B. Janeczko • Scholastic Teaching Resources

Organizer: Personification

Fill in the organizer below by listing "person" qualities and "object" qualities.

"Person" Qualities	Object Qualities

Organizer: Alliteration

Fill in the organizer below with some examples of alliteration that you notice in everyday life.

Stores/Products	Advertising
Entertainment	**Conversation**

Teaching Literary Elements Using Poetry © 2014 by Paul B. Janeczko • Scholastic Teaching Resources

Teaching Literary Elements Using Poetry © 2014 by Paul B. Janeczko • Scholastic Teaching Resources

Name _____ Date _____

Organizer: Onomatopoeia

Complete the organizer below with examples of onomatopoeia—noise words. For each word, list what might make that sound.

Noise Word	What makes that sound?

Name _____ Date _____

Organizer: Mask Poem

List five things that the washing machine claims that it does when it works. Mark the two spots where the washing machine speaks metaphorically.

1.	
2.	
3.	
4.	
5.	

Teaching Literary Elements Using Poetry © 2014 by Paul B. Janeczko • Scholastic Teaching Resources

Name _____   Date _____

Organizer: Mood

Choose some moods. Then list words you feel might create that mood.

Mood _____	Mood _____	Mood _____
Mood _____	Mood _____	Mood _____

Name _____ Date _____

Organizer: Poetic Patterns

Fill in the organizer below with examples of poetic patterns.

Sound	Repetition
Stanza	**Length of Line**

Teaching Literary Elements Using Poetry © 2014 by Paul B. Janeczko • Scholastic Teaching Resources

Glossary

Alliteration Alliteration is the repetition of initial consonant sounds.

Character A character is a person or other figure in a work of literature.

Characterization Characterization is how the writer reveals what a character is like.

Climax Climax is the exciting point in the story where the main character or characters face and make a huge decision.

Figurative Language Figurative language refers to any language that uses images or language that makes different kinds of comparisons. Examples of figurative language include metaphor, simile, and personification.

Metaphor A metaphor is a word or phrase that compares one thing to another without use of the words *like* or *as*. Metaphors are not factually true, but they help readers see events and characters in a vivid way.

Mood Mood is the atmosphere or general feeling in a work of literature. Writers create atmosphere by using imagery and descriptions.

Onomatopoeia Onomatopoeia refers to the use of words that sound like the objects they name or the sounds these objects make, like *tick-tock*, *quack*, *moo*, and *buzz*.

Personification Personification is a type of metaphor in which human qualities are given to something that is not human, such as a tree or a car.

Plot Plot is the series of related events that make up the story. Most plots involve solving a conflict.

Poetic Patterns Poetic patterns are structural repetition found most often in rhyming poems. Examples include repetition of sound, such as rhythm and rhyme, and length of lines or stanzas.

Point of View The point of view in a literary work is the vantage point from which the story is told.

Setting Setting is where and when a poem or story takes place.

Simile A simile is a comparison that compares two unlike things and in which the words *like* or *as* are used.

Symbolism Symbolism uses an object to stand for something larger than itself.

Theme Theme is the big idea or lesson that a story conveys about life. The writer usually doesn't state the theme directly. It's up to readers to discover the theme for themselves.

Tone Tone is the attitude or style of expression used in writing. Writers choose words and images to create a story's tone.

Teaching Literary Elements Using Poetry © 2014 by Paul B. Janeczko • Scholastic Teaching Resources

Notes

Teaching Literary Elements Using Poetry © 2014 by Paul B. Janeczko • Scholastic Teaching Resources

CPSIA information can be obtained
at www.ICGtesting.com
Printed in the USA
LVHW060732180722
723725LV00009B/142